Other books by Rudolph von Abele

Alexander H. Stephens: A Biography

*The Death of the Artist: A Study in
Hawthorne's Disintegration*

The Vigil of Emmeline Gore—a novel

The Party—a novel

A Cage
for
Loulou

Drawing by Belisario R. Contreras

A Cage for Loulou

Poems by

RUDOLPH VON ABELE

LOUISIANA STATE UNIVERSITY PRESS

Baton Rouge and London

1978

Copyright © 1978 by Rudolph von Abele
All rights reserved

Designer: Albert Crochet
Type face: VIP Palatino
Typesetter: Graphic World, Inc., St. Louis, Missouri
Printer and binder: Thomson-Shore, Dexter, Michigan

LIBRARY OF CONGRESS CATALOGING IN PUBLICATION DATA

Von Abele, Rudolph Radama, 1922–
    A cage for Loulou.

    I. Title.
PS3572.0417C3   811'.5'4   77–17394
ISBN 0–8071–0382–9
ISBN 0–8071–0383–7

*This book is for all those
without whom not*

Contents

ONE

Variations on a
Paradox

Poet Counterpoet

How peaceful to have been Li-Po, lying back
drunk in a boat, without oars, among reeds,
remarking the strange truth that his arms
were clasping themselves behind his head, and
that the moon was moving in the sky: to have

been Li-Po, inventing verses, inventing verses
about Li-Po, lying back, drunk in a boat, without
oars, among reeds, at home with the moon and
with his arms, telling himself aloud that what
he made in yellow drunkenness would be revised

in blue sobriety, moon-flimmer, insects, reeds
shushing about time, his arms, the oars, the suede
surface of the river. . . . And then to be Li-Po,
or to pretend to be Li-Po, sitting upright, dead
sober, strapped into the down-screaming fiery plane,

studying the Jersey Meadows, puzzling out how
to invent verses about Li-Po, studying the Jersey
Meadows from a plane, all that lackluster broom-
grass, those sulfuric ponds, those caved-in
factories, those rusting cars craned one atop

the other, making jagged love, dead sober, and the
impossible geometry of pipes and railroad tracks,
those sour man-breaths stilling up into the regions
of the moon from dumps among the grass, among the
ponds, and to wish oneself drunkward among reeds. . . .

Moons and Caves

At the joint convention of astronauts and speleologists
there was vague agreement but not much communication.

The mind is a cave; the moon, a woman. Caves are damp,
down-bearing, chilly, light-lacking, and hung with drapery

of bats. The moon is airless, powdery, hot and cold by turns,
and it makes saltimbanques of men who try to master it.

Metaphors are true and not true, take them leave them.
The convention met in a padded ballroom rented from the press

3

club. If you liked, you could look out the windows during
speeches. The world, that day, was big with wind, the few trees

visible kept trying genuflections; and at the end a flea-
fat and blood-sucking sun was floating in a gloria of shifting

clouds. You could say yes, well, caves of the earth or
deserts of the moon, it is all one, doctors of silver for unwary

fish that never learn. . . . At the convention they all wore
lapel badges, loitered at the bar, shook hands, exchanged

remarks, laughed, and from time to time remembered what was
real. So up is up and down is down and level is where

Aristotle lives. That night, they tangled chopsticks in
communal soup, groping for pork, affirming each other's amiability.

After that convention ended, one observer went to his motel
and would have hanged himself, except for this: the hook was loose.

But still, the real estate of man is such that any sensitive
proprietor ought to find the form and file for bankruptcy.

Skutchno na etom svete, gospoda

There is a kind of ice will not melt even in the jungle.
The man encapsulated is looking at what goes on and on.
What goes on and on is this and that flies buzzing in spilled beer.
A wounded soldier's breath blows no dust from the moon.
The man encapsulated feels like the moon reflecting soldiers.

If the ice were startled into melting would the man sweat salt?

It is just as well that the ice is guaranteed impregnable.
It has been manufactured to decline all temperatures equally.
So the soldier dies and the moon is littered with brain children.
And what goes on and on is this and that rain blur against the window.
The scenario is then a still life in the strictest sense.

Astronomer's Complaint

The red shift in
the galaxies
impoverishes the mind

4

windily between your fractured fangs old
dandelion head

Flap flap went Crow toward the soft sun
squat Squirrel on
his wall peeled to himself a something
green reward

Let girls and boys go make together under
Jesus hanging skies
drawn onward by eternal murmuring of plum
Malvolio hears thunder

Stendhal Beyle Brûlard

and the two hundred other pseudonyms he took
to throw Linnaeus off the scent of his family:
wrote "imgo ingt obef if ty" in was it red
ink in the elastic band inside his trousers:

scribbled with his stick in sand the encoded
letters designating all the women he had loved:
by subscript indicating those he had possessed
once or twice in a life of endless perseverance:

detesting Paris he wanted to be buried elsewhere
under the insulting truth "Arrigo Beyle Milanese:
visse amo scrisse" but had to drop dead on a Paris
street and so was boneyarded in Père-Lachaise:

que voulez-vous, ce serait la dernière blague
for one who hated grocers priests and Sunday:
all that Grenoble blood drunk on memories of
horses flames snow emperors epaulettes and war:

and those reverberant soft velvet boudoirs of
the senses woman after woman mirroring enticement:
diffident fat provincial with a mind whenever he
could reach the goal he booked it in his diary

Satie

There is the inventor of the absinthe sandwich.
I have come to die with you he used to whisper
There is the matchbox Valhalla for the nightingale
But in the end they had to come to die with him

There is a general
drifting away so I
should open an echoing

gallery we have not
practiced shivering
an exercise like others

Heeltaps and voices
and they too exemplify
a drift but toward

the violet invisible
nightly two by two
they float away away

Two is the most fear-
ful number always
busy just try dialing it

Binaries make for hope
for they revolve
around a mutual center

and every night
the lights come on
and then go off

When I was younger I
never knew how cold
observatories have to be

Excuses

Well, to be born before your time or
to be born

too late, or to be born on schedule—
which no one is—

exhausts our possibilities, except
of course not

to be born at all at all at all at all,
or so said *panie*

Sofokles, that displaced Dubliner, smiling
among the ruins of Warsaw

like an American general with cheeks akimbo.
After you, Herr Scipio

Aemilianus Africanus, razor of cities. . . .
Before him, God knows who.

A happy poem about peace and love and beauty
would be, I swear,

a grand event entirely, but all that I can
say is out of Plato:

Paradise is closed to poets, since the putting
greens there grow not

nor do they wither, hence what need for men
in white to mow

or men in fashionable black to fertilize and
couple up the sprinklers?

—O well, Saint Brendan was Saint Brendan and I
am I, but what did he find

that was so wonderful? Far back in Warsaw
are still the faithful poor.

The Prevalence of Guilt

The past is not beneath us in the bulby earth.
The past is overhead, it comes as beaks of birds
    diving at the fontanelles.

Time no hot chariot, eternity no desert be.
Shuffle we so, plain foot by peppermint pajama,
    for to flat we to black wall.

Like a bush porter in lush wallet sepia,
I tote, strapped to my spine, my human bed,
    spooring the ungodly monuments.

Gun take away we ghost, by much of blood.
Picture box eye eat up we bone for bullet head,
    look he at, he have big glad.

The salt beaks slobber for the taste of brain.
Under these callused hooves, the earth yeasts up
    wet dreams of leaf and fruit.

Enfin (with apologies to Christin

hallucinated lunch in the Speisesaal w
lounging gaseously concertina talk of

when are they good when bad and et
about how flying saucers on the plate

ideas of peupler le système solaire fro
Earth con smitstof that likes to call its

while someone is it I keeps toiling up
ziggurat toward the Pfarrer on the for

into the mouth of a spøgelse droning
aber auf dem Tischtuch as the 747 vib

with a slow malrapide fastness violati
a gross sebaceous Gesicht among les

zooms personally me-ward like a fly
takes on the third dimension shooting

rasch straight for my pulpy heart as I
with a beer and vaguely auskultis ab

when are they good when bad among
gaseously large and small in the unde

Fabula Morosa

Crow came down on the concret
and hunched himself
and Squirrel whose wall it really
made furiously

This blue sky opens wide like Jes
the sun intones
after old manners and all that bu
discourages me

So Squirrel chittered tail and tee
and raced along
his wall but Crow sat lumpy and
and Squirrel fled

One proof of Paradise is not to d
go blow that

There is the glass coffin gliding on a tricycle.
Opening his door for them by pulling on a rope
There is the fall of hammers auctioning his olive pits.
That ran over a pulley in the ceiling to his hand
There is the unsanitary belt of his old salty muse.
Where he sat like a rooster huddling eggs of pain.
There is the inventor of the humours of our evenings.

Dublin Poems

I   Aubade

As long as I have been sojourning in this city,
I have listened with pleasure to the crying
of its birds in the air: spooks or caretakers,
I cannot say which; perhaps even prophets.

I have watched them under all skies rising
high over chimneys, or bending toward the river
to rest on the rough stones of the parapets,
or floating into the pungent asparagus-broth

under the bridges, dipping for food. But only
once have I heard what I heard at five o'clock
one morning, bursting up out of my thicket
of dreams to run to the window to see

what bird could have uttered that death-cry
that had driven its beak through my eyelids.
I leaned out and listened: the cry was being
dragged up from green guts by a rusted hook

on a chain wound on a windlass. Was it because
it was ear-shy, or because it needed all
the strength it could get to tear itself out
through the slender spout of the neck? Whatever

the reason, that cry, already too dark
for the mind, seemed to be groining itself inward,
and to grow darker and thickly embedded,
like a car sunk in the silt of the river,

whose doll-jointed occupants sway as though
trying to help the grappling-hooks loosen them
lightward. I leaned far out and looked,
as far as I could see, into the damp dawn:

but found only a courtyard of blank bricks
and glass, half an orange face down on a skylight.
After a time, the crying loudly broke off,
and then tried to begin again, but couldn't.

II   Four Movements of Anna Liffey

1   *Chapelizod*

And on an unsettled day I climbed down from the bus
and walked a few hundred yards to the west past a church
and a pub, and, wheeling a corner downhill and downwind,
saw beyond the compacted roof-lines of a family of houses
long flattened hair of hillsides being combed green,
and came to what seemed like a bridge on which
I paused and leaned over and looked along the water,
which was dark and clean and responsive to the wind,
flowing alongside the houses, and I began taking pictures
but was doubtful, this water being so narrow, and when
a young man came by I asked him was this indeed the Liffey
and he told me yes and I said that it did not much
resemble itself when in town and he smiled and agreed
and went on, and I crossed to the upstream side
of the bridge and went on taking pictures of clarity
and of quick and fugitive movement, cold and dark
under low leaf-heavy trees, knowing it was really no use,
and then walked on a bit and turned back, sniffing clean air
and listening to the wind, and thinking how at this point
all was indeed innocence, and considering the influences
on the way to the sea that would turn this water of life
into slow supersaturated bile sumping between quays,
and how this dark child gaily unknowing would break
and run past Islandbridge and the weirs and past Heuston
only to come short up between in-closing sea-hairy arms.

2   *Ellis Quay*

At ebb tide this poor river has to confess itself
to a cloud-wrangled sky too busy to hear it.

A brownish-green oil draws down from the blackening
walls of the prison to which men have remanded it.

Limp seaweed overripe for the carding slumps in and out
of a quibble of upended prams and milk-bottle carriers.

By the big toe at the end of the curve of the bridge-foot
a sluice of something tawny undisturbs an eddy of gulls.

The cries of these birds rise with their white wings
as they manoeuver among rocks bared to the gums.

This water has been hemmed in for too many years,
and it faintly chafes as if it wanted to go somewhere else.

But the indifferent backhand of the sea keeps playing it
up and down along across the court defined by the quays.

And when the tide is at flood the black and green beards
of these walls are drowned in a coordinate trance.

Then the brownish-green oil stands up high in the bottle
wrinkling itself like the slow skin of an old man's face.

Opaque as a skin and resembling a syrup that brewers reject
this thick water repels the inquisitive visiting eye.

Which merely confirms that it must have something to hide
so that there is at no time any escape from confession.

All day a long march of dependable clouds takes place
while the river fluctuates between its high and low truths.

3   Sir John Rogerson's Quay

Along the grey quay-clatter the freighters roll slowly
and slowly yield like animals being unburdened or burdened.

The cranes riding their quadruped gantries dangle fat hooks
or if working swing and stop and swing again smoothly.

Here the river begins to become less sure of itself
for it is already turning into a finger of the sea probing.

Of a color as yet undecided it suffers the intrusions
of ships that enter it sperm-shaped and making long tracks.

On both flanks bounded it shifts as though obeying the will
of the man at a smudged window shortly docketing invoices.

There is bright blue slashed into its oleaginous green
but bright is still mainly for things men put paint on.

White meal of Snowcrete in bundles of sacks puffs out
as the claw of a crane climbs up from a low yellow belly.

And a thick man in a forklift angrily spears
a navy-grey barrel of stout and shuttles it eastward.

Another man in a forklift furiously pirouettes the barrel
to where a ship's winch raises and lowers it like an arm.

So concrete comes in and Guinness' goes out from Liverpool
to Liverpool in freighters crossing the wind-rubbed Moyle.

Or you might say just as well from Blackpool to Blackpool
since what goes on is exchange in the most literal sense.

Along an alphabet of stooping buildings a freshness is born
here at the slack mouth of her where she begins ending.

4   The Pigeon House

And as a last gift from the city she has to take in
a freshet of sewage creaming up like stout in the glass
from the outfall works just west of the Pigeon House,
and the tall stack letting off a brown feather of smoke,
but it no longer matters for by now she is very far gone
and altogether losing her self, and one way you can tell
is by the blueness and the skylarking of her under the wind
that blows up the big bags of clouds suddenly driving you
hard to the wall of a building for shelter from cold rain
that is over as violently as it came on, and commends
to the morning sun the patient roofs shining with wet,
and so when you ask about buses the young redheaded man
tells you no you can't go any farther and there aren't
many buses and "you better just trot on up the road now,"
tapping you on the shoulder as if to emphasize a sly point,
and the men clumped from the shower in the angle of a wall
come back out to their jackhammers, and as you turn back
breasting a tumult of air and delighting in on your right
the blue blue of the laxative Bay, a freighter glides past
and is gone to unload the oranges and apples from Sydney
and Jaffa you smelled the day before in Mary's Lane market
to be eaten by children whose pictures you took in Chapelizod,
and athwart the never-still empty wide water the shoreline
lies scrawled of the North Bull and Dollymount and farther
northeastward heavily low as befits the head of a giant
the wreathed Hill of Howth sleeps under burred shadow-lights.

III   Four Bagatelles

1   *A Sort of a Ballad*

The brown hair of the girls of this city runs down
    over their shoulders
but the water runs down over the lips of the locks
    of disused canals.

And wonder of wonders I saw on a wide morning of clouds
    two ancient swans
pick lice from their feathers where they were standing
    in the muck of the Dodder.

Beds of elaborate flowers are disposed in the gardens
    and the trees are green
but the color of walls in this city of walls is grey
    and even the sky makes a wall.

2   *An Apparition*

Riding the top of the bus on my way back
from Sandycove, I could not stop watching
a dropsical elderly man whose great head
kept falling forward into his arms
that hung like sacks over the top of the seat
in front of him, and french-fried fingers
he kept letting be scorched by a cigarette,
which would, for a moment, revive him.

To travel that way is dangerous, without
a mother to take it in and hide it
away from us, the waterlogged foetus
with adipose eyelids and undisciplined belly
that pouts like an underlip outward,
and a head that keeps falling forward
because, being in love with its toes,
it cannot bear to kiss them goodbye.

3   *A Vision*

Aimlessly walking the streets after having studied
at Charlemont House a show

of contemporary paintings, I felt an odd exultation
at this discovery—

four children's sandals without any feet in them, posed
pigeon-toed on the stones
of the pavement not far from the Communist bookshop
in Essex Street, and looking

as if they had been left there by a pair of ascending
putti, like those of whom
the chubby heads are stuck pertly through the ceiling
of the Rotunda Hospital

chapel, amused and indifferent and with an effect
of floating like gulls over
the Liffey, over the city, as if they could find nothing
below to warrant disclosing their bodies.

4 *Comment on a Comment*
for Ed Kessler

"Life," he said, "for me is an affair
of places not people": and there is
a beauty that can hardly be argued

in a street of shut doors and drawn blinds
on a morning of clouds, and nobody there,
only the bang of a bell in a steeple,
and a quick smell of coal-smoke, as if

someone sequestered had lifted the lid
off a kettle on an iron stove, and then
put it back, a witch behind gingerbread.

It seems all for a moment so spacious
without that slick feeling of eels
in a basket, but of course it is false,
and as a crowd of girls chatters out

of a convent, a street-sweeper shoving
his cart round the corner is passed
by an elderly cyclist winding himself

workward, and from behind a white
curtain, itself behind the glass of a tall
window set in a house built of brick, a hand
appears, gently watering flowers.

IV   Envoi

The music he was making sounded mostly for the eye,
a rude archaic body-language hammering out
the tousled swarthy truculence of those who, sagging
to their knees, keep struggling to hold themselves

upright, by help if necessary of the shoulder-blade
stone railing of O'Connell Bridge, into which
his backside-bones pressed, while his torso
swayed without stopping, to fro to fro, besotted

vagrant beast lumbering nowhere to the windings
of the drowned tunes his fists squeezed from the pleats.
Behind him, a long sun bummeled down into over
the Four Courts coiling clouds: and the river

breathed, up down up down, an exercise in prison
discipline. Before, melisma of green-and-yellow buses
underscored the evensong of workers eagering toward
a fanged mouth, six o'clock, gammon or plaice, potatoes,

in Palmerston, Stillorgan, Santry, Sutton, Castleknock,
and afterward the telly and the pub, suburb without end.
Nobody paid him any heed, no coins dropped flat
into the flyspecked box beside his brogues: he might

as well have been an eleemosynary singer, singing
only because not to sing would let death have the city,
or ratify the death already there in guise
of all that pullulation among dangerous buildings.

The fierceness in him was not just in his movements
but also in his voice, flattened at the poles, abrupt,
and surly as those are whose used-up bodies sense
and half-accept the fibrillated wounds of centuries

of life along the knife's edge: but even so secrete
a seedy pride that sends out shoots, grows fingers
of deceptive humor, continually opening and shutting,
slily murderous, around the ungovernable neck of history.

Dublin: June, 1972

Am I Not Your Son?

Years and years we met in silence after my Bible class,
and walked in silence to the drug store,
picked up the *Times* in silence, and in silence went home.

How peaceful and false the odor of your pipe—I too
by the way have taken to smoking now—
as you sat with your stiff back to the window's glare,

scanning and laying aside, methodically, section by
section, the Word of the world, until
the clock struck three, when you stood up, sighed, knocked

the ashes out, tuned in the Philharmonic, and put the water
on for the inevitable *Kaffeeklatsch*.
We practice lifting stones with forks of lead. . . . Old man,

old man, my father, listen to me now, even though your ears
are deaf, and we have so poor a tongue:
eighty-three years are vanished from your one sad life,

yet still you shuffle fearfully from mark to mark to mark
around the face of the gold watch your
father cursed you with, as if you might be late for dying.

Or is it that death, for you, was always the end of school?
But how am I to blame you that you claimed my *me*
where it sat puzzling itself among the uncompleted bones?

Some Realizations Come Suddenly

To hear a mind go, that is a frightening thing,
like watching a church being blown up in slow
motion, or as if a stone went rotten between
the fingers, and holes like pores appeared
and stared at you with angry eyes, as if
it was your fault that here comes crazy death!
Soft, too, like runny cheese, and those
abrupt discontinuities, how do you jump them?

The dwarf clown in the carny show, walking
head down across a muddy field or sitting
in a booth alone behind his untouched coke,
what would he tell the grandson he will never
have, when he is eighty-four, without his mask,

hating the spry birds flirting on the sill,
an eye in every one of his arthritic bones,
and the nurse comes in with the assembled lunch?

For many years I wadded up my mind against
my father's monologues about his past, his family,
the wealth and names and titles history
danced away with like a gay tornado, and now
that he is dead I have become like a museum
to him, noticing without surprise how I consult
his watch, write with his pen, and study out
the lineaments of all those portraits in my veins.

Requiem for a Persian. My Mother's Birthday.

Out walking on a Sunday afternoon,
the last in March, I stopped
because the grey-haired woman standing
at the extreme edge of her property
looked so angry, glaring at the street.
Behind her, two children slowly moved

across the lawn, carrying a makeshift
bier on which the cat lay, so I
was told, for at that distance
it was hard to see. Going silently
before, a third child, holding high
a sterling candelabrum, I was told,

borrowed for this one occasion
only, no doubt from the mahogany
sideboard in the dining-room.
The silver softly glowed. Three
specks of fire burned yellow
in the quiet air. The day was quiet

but overcast. Slow and solemn,
the children paced their yard, a mat
of brown just coming back to life,
and vanished around the house. He
was a Persian, I was told, four
years of age, eighteen pounds, prize

of a pure-bred litter, beautiful.
I listened to the children singing.

Whoever hit him was going over
the speed limit, not to be able or not
to care to stop, slow down, or even
swerve. People, I was told, are always

coming up that street too fast.
The woman's finger pointed. I turned
to look. The concrete, it was true,
was indeed smeared with a dull red
which might have been either blood or paint.
I had not noticed it before. From

behind the house, the children were
chanting something all together in a jumble.
Having buried, they now would mourn him. . . .
That Sunday was my mother's birthday.
I had just talked with her an hour
before. Her body's health, I understood,

was reasonably good, but she was cloudier
than ever in her mind. She kept
forgetting that it was her birthday,
confusing the ages of my children,
and could not remember when she last had
seen my wife. While my eyes remarked

that the red smears in the street were dry,
my mind smiled to think—but paint
would not so easily wash out with rain—
that my mother had already forgotten
both that I had remembered to call her up
and that she herself was truly eighty-four.

Graz, in the Summer of 1957

Night after night, in that moth month of August,
while your mother was elsewhere, I made you stories
    of Pedro Tavès, grand adventurer.
I lugged them up, slippery and green, out of the cold
undulations of my all-at-sea, and made them feasts

to stuff your gluttonous ears, which might have heard
unholy sounds. One night a mixed-up bat came whirling
    through the open window-dark.
We shooed him out again, a little scared, a little sad.
Pedro's career along the dusty highroads of the mind

was not for him, disoriented and minutely crying
the way a butterfly might beat and beat its wings, a
     butterfly burst from a fire.
A woman in a raincoat pasted hairs across the wood slats
of our coal bin down in the cellar, so as to find out

when Someone would remove the corpse she claimed was in
our trunk. Head down, she paced among the minefields
     when it rained, to tempt her enemies.
It was a hard time, what with microphones in light bulbs,
Russian bombers diving down upon the house, and agents

signaling between the hills by making windows lightly wink.
It ended when she walked with me to the white ward,
     the two-faced men, the insulin.
She did not know she was going there, but just before
we arrived, she wanted to sit down beside a pond

of floating ducks and grasses, where we drank two pale
mélanges at a table, under a pale sun of late July, and
     then went on, up to the end.
After that delivery, old Pedro Tavès, hero of my comic
strip, began, that ancient child, his brief engagement,

Don Punchinello in the mask of Parsifal, fumbling up
salvation tips from secret pockets, acting all the old
     pratfalls, all the usual escapes.
You and your sister turned into brats, that month, annoying
fussy ladies while I snipped the long path with my legs,

descending every queasy afternoon to reason with unreason
in the *Landeskrankenhaus*, although I could not comprehend,
     I, foreigner, its black patois.
And we, we sauntered among the trees at noon, and took
a table in the garden of the *Wirtshaus*, where you drank

Chabesade, and I dark beer, and all of us ate schnitzel,
Rotkraut, Rostkartoffeln. And in the end we went away. We
     could have stayed, but didn't.
I judged it pointless. So did Pedro Tavès, for he died.
I fished and fished, far down my all-at-sea, fingering

slick stones and old wet hairs, but there was no one.
Pedro had returned to the deeper country he had come from.
     We went away and did not look behind.
It was a time of bitterness and angry beds and wranglefear.
It lasted long: as long as the moment between death and death.

—Remember Pedro Tavès then, who rose and fell in one month,
whose raffish chronicle kept us alive among the stolid
    people, among the whirlingness,
Pedro, who scavenged for, and found, a kind of Grail. Remember
all your evenings the healing power of a foolish poem.

About That of Which One Cannot Speak,
One Must Be Silent

The day of the eclipse, I took my daughter
to her small "rock park" down the street,
so as to find us each a proper station
from which to watch the woman moon of night
working to calm her husband's heat
by crossing him at just his fury's zenith.

I am no enemy to life, yet once I
scrupulously focused on a yellow spider
the German burning-glass my father
had given me for having done well in
arithmetic, until, quite stopped, eight legs
curled up around a shriveled belly.

Another time, beside the sea, stripped
to combustible and raunchy skin, in the soft
gullet of a dune, as shadows shrank away,
I drowsed, abandoned by the only one who
might have wakened me, so that I had to smolder
two weeks running on a solitary bed.

A little girl, head down, jumps carefully
among uneven, shadowed, spectral stones,
while an arrested man, his face up-tilted,
stained by a violet radiance in the sky,
warns her to look and not to look,
to keep a tree between her and the sun.

Are Roses Red in the Dark?

The stone lies at the bottom of the pool.

If a child, wandering by, should pause,
and stir the water with a broken stick,
aimlessly, as children will,

21

opening a round eye in a web of green,
the stone might seem to beat,
might seem
to beat like a dislocated heart
awakened to the feeling: once, I was alive.

There is the first dilemma of philosophy.
At most, we may propound: no toads are princes,
although some princes may be toads.
Why should a sleeping hand
keep opening and closing on itself?
A bequest of sunlight and clean air is called for.

In the end,
having lost interest,
flinging the broken stick into the tall grass,
the child, aimlessly, as children will,
would move away
through a soft rain of insects, while,
the round eye very slowly closing,
the water would grow still again.

And nothing would have happened to the stone.

Die Welt ist alles, was der Fall ist

If he still knows his name he has to
hang onto it with both hands clenched.
As a young boy I had to grip
the dripping sea-slimed rope
when waves came climbing toward me
on heavy mornings after storms,
and the bottom insidiously kept
changing shape between my toes.

Like a baby bird's, all trust and
hunger, his eyes expect from me.
—Are you the doctor, I throwed up
all my breakfast this morning,
must be I got stomach cancer.—
Out too far a yard and I would
start to slip down over my head.
I hated that salt water in my nose.

Open the screen door, walk down
the steps.—Gimme a quarter, I

need a pack of cigarettes, I'll pay
you back, I'm a good boy.—Rising,
a soft claw begs of my sleeve, while
under a stained hat peaked just
like a leprechaun's, the eyes
keep offering themselves to me.

But I can't want his eyes!—God
bless you doc, I'll pray for you,
(*conspiratorial*), you know I got
a wife upstairs, you pray for me.—
The claw flings benedictions vaguely
wifeward. I think, how many kinds of
stairs, and at the head of each a wife?
— You ain't the doctor, are you,

I seen you yesterday, I'll pay
you back, God bless you, doc, pray
for me, I'll pray for you, have I
got cancer, listen, I been good.—
And lifts my hand to bless it with a kiss.
The beach was best when most
uneasy, for then it was deserted,
no man to shame me, plunging

straight into the glass curves
of aggressive crests. Contracted
as with pain, he scuttles across the
steaming lawn, zigzagging traps
laid for him alone. Walk on then,
carrying my beard the way
a doctor should. I think: I have
been here too often. Unlike a doctor,

I look back. No use, he has
already vanished around the corner
of the porch, where a black man in
a blue shirt beats on the grillwork
—O Lord I want out O Lord I want
out—collapsing to a mumble as a
joyless phonograph treads in its track.
Walk on, I feel too personally

involved. A wave once took me under,
and my palms, after it had thrown
me up again, kept bleeding blood
into the surf, because my fingers would

not let go the rope. My ears rang
red, salt stunned my eyes, my nose
was stuffed with sand, I ached for days.
One must, one must respect the sea.

A Parable

Ill with darkest illness, he had lain a long
while deathly still, saying nothing, disdaining
nourishment, locking his senses up against the world.
He seemed engrossed in sensing of the in-himself.

One afternoon, just before sundown, he sat up,
smiled, spoke, gave gestures, and began alluding
to the future. He sketched out startling baroque
landscapes of extraordinary human festivals.

They stared at one another, feeling warmth, at
him, recalling Lazarus. They let his amplitude
and princely ease enfold them like a chasuble.
And they sailed with him high into the grand winds.

That night, he died. It was not that the vistas
were maladroitly rendered, nor that the logic
of the spirit lacked validity. All his prospects
were, simply, the false final flaring of old fire.

Variations on a Paradox

1

All your life you keep on hunting
in the dark

the pen with which to scrawl the great equation
between words and life.

All your life you keep on learning
in the dark

that words are words and life is life that words
are life and life is words.

You keep on stumbling through the old house
in the dark

displacing furniture and listening to cold rain
gurgle in the downspouts.

2

The final human utterances are so simple—
the infant's cry, being born,
the hurt man's cry of pain,
the lover's cry.

That we must make poems is a perplexity:
why does the mind keep worrying
the final utterances as if they
had no tongues?

3

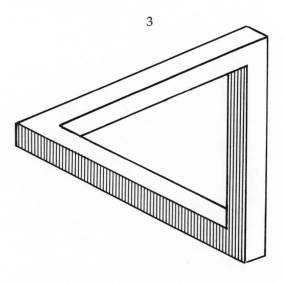

TWO

The Loulou
Poems

I

New Year Letter
for Molloy

Les Adieux, in Retrograde

A point, a point, it swells and zooms
into the awaited handshake,
and, as suddenly, from sweaty palm to oily finger-
tip, going going gone, diminishes itself, a point
again,
as a music will move inside the time the head holds.

All pain is of the body, which does
all the thinking too, poor gallused fool,
snapping his braces alongside some black highway, thumbing
a ride, but the big rigs and the cars alike keep sailing
by.
After a day of rain, sometimes there is that wound,

that parting of the clouds, letting the fire through,
to be glimpsed, coveted, extinguished. The
points, so metamathematical, wax and wane, absently be-
getting flowers all but graspable, handsels to be known, with
love.
But the power of perspective seems too much for us.

Da Capo, Trying for Al Fine

:   Recovery of the feeling of the feeling of the
scene, as it appears, just now, after the storm,
to have appeared to seem to feel (no laughter),
back then, when we were locked in struggle far
beneath, a sliver of a shade above the slime: is
that the final assignment. . . . ? *You* decide. I
am advertising for an unused anacoustic chamber,
I hate these whispering galleries. How else am I
to listen to my own voice, without interference?

But who is I, who you? The weather clearing off,
over oceans of rising falling multicolored water,
a salt sun being shoved along, and the obligatory
gulls hovering high up over the below-there,
the fish just out of reach, it makes a model to be
studied (in a poem perhaps?). But to bear the tension
between two faces is, at times, more than the
others forced into the fracas are able to endure.
And neither facing face, inhabiting its cruelties,

can grasp this. It would be flattering indeed
to wring polite applause from an audience of hired
mannikins set down to sway along the beach, tossing
straw hats in silence, crumpling back into their
pockets their blood-stained handkerchiefs, lining
up to collect their easy pay (disbursed by whom?).
What will we not do, to shame this mundane world
that bears us! . . . But look at the picked metaphor.
What justifies the choice of an aqueous vehicle

to carry a tenor breaking on the high F of failure?
(Obscene gestures.) It is the present moment
that I wish to re-create, before it has a chance
to happen incorrectly. Swinging away, ears
cocked to foam of fresher music, opening the silted
senses—so much is true, the accidental vision,
so far down under, so blurred by undulant striations,
stirs up old hungers. It is so. Well, let them
starve. A swimmer found himself, once, in the deep

water: Describe his cry. "Blundering off against
the blinding glare of freedom, which he could not see,
rebellious in cowardice, he had to—" (No; not this.)
Redundant signals, aspiring too high, bounce off
against the baffles of a dampened past. And that
is the irrecoverable feeling of the feeling of the scene,
now, then, there, when, here, where, a wet brain
slashing, an embattled king, a tantalizing sea, a sea,
and naturally failing. . . . I, at least, must hear myself :

Memorial

It stroked itself against the mucus of the heart
until the irritation called for wiping. Then the hand,

pleasurably flattered, responsive, made connections.
It was as if what one had thought to be a gnat had
turned out, captured and closely inspected, an esoteric
moth with a platonic genealogy. . . . The light was feeble.
Iridescence, in course of time, invariably fibrillates

itself. All regions are exotic, until you travel them,
if you linger long enough to read the cockroaches.
—You might of course have stayed at home, that day.
There were, as you knew, forecasts of thundershowers.
And the terrain was unfamiliar. But, but, once
that move was made, the creature clung, and clung, and
kissed. A kitten in the snow, what does one do about it?

And how is one to recognize the jaguar in the egg,
if one is ignorant of embryology? The blind are interdict
from running stop signs. Breasts, on the other hand, are
contours to them. Safety is relative. And if your gnat
shows fangs, or if your kitten mauls the hand that
feeds it? . . . Should you survive, under the lamp, alone,
before the reassuring mirror, make shift to thank your self.

New Year Letter for Molloy

"The year begins, that sour meal." Sit down to it.
"But the last has not yet done digesting, let alone
   the antepenultimate disaster, or the holy mess heaped

up beneath that one, or the iron coils of turd
beyond. . . ." So hold apart the cheeks, and strain:
expel, into the void, these bloody distillations.

"Dawn is a dismal interregnum. . . ." Yes yes, here
comes the classic landskip, frigid weeds, ice-
lacquered, glistening as if to please Nobody's eye,

not to speak of Night's disease, paling into color,
paling off the still world, paling in the sun,
and the birds too, paradigmatists of folly, sharply

probing frozen dirt. . . . "But this has all happened
a billion times!" Yes. Hunched and shivering, you will
squat on the back steps of your brain, inventing it.

Tendentious Picture of the Exhibition of an Exhibition

Cats with mice, and dogs with bones, and people
with each other: there is a pleasure in it.
With people, it may be, the sex counts most—
not the gender, for that, we know, is inculcated,
but the simplistic straw-haired sex, that will
not be subservient, restrained, correct, like Bunter,
but insists on rising up, like Banquo, to disrupt

the feast. . . . All these machines, so much devoutly
polished metal, so regularly moving, or so still,
and all these humans straying among the objects,
objects themselves, yearning for objects in the stillness,
in the movement, in the genial pedal-points
that lock up and put away the time in which a seedling
might push up, the moment in which a kiss might

foster complications. . . . They desire a certainty,
sure knowledge of the future, in which sex loses heart,
being too akin to passion, swallowed up by a smooth
carpentry of terror that equalizes all humanity
under the guillotine. No: it is true, no guillotine
is here. But everywhere the ghost of time-and-
motion study hovers, withering the fantailed palms.

Repetitiveness kneads the flesh. And every valve
must open at its predetermined instant, and also shut.
On these crowds milling among these aisles, the girls,
the girls, the men, the women, the women, the women,
the children, the boys, the boys, the spectacle
affirms itself, a lesson in the virtues of redundancy. . . .
So love before breakfast curdles into breakfast

without love, a blue Niagara of decontaminated pellets.
The god who dominates us here is immanent. Bodies
dissolve before him, flow like hot iron down along
determined channels, to be cast into chilled parts.
The gospel of interchangeability will get us nowhere.
And the old fury that love must flame up out of
is absent from this circus, so organized, so epicene.

Washington, May 1976

Will the Black Watch Hesitate to Shoot?

1

It is said that the hunter loves the beast he kills.
Wilde may have had that sort of thing in mind.
At least, it seems most valid when hunter and beast
are one, and the hard barrel is deep inside the mouth.
Still, the contrary may be just as true: who knows?
And neither view means anything to those who died.

Ahhh. . . ! One grows weary of all this blather about
love and death. One wearies of all that misconstrued
fellatio, those spent miscarriages spattering the morgue.
And what if Kronos swallowed all his get but one?
By river-banks, on bad streets, at the backs of spongy
meadows, from attic-beams or shower-heads, guarded,

unguarded, deliberate, fortuitous, out of pentecostal
malice or misdirected sorrow, with shotgun, tranquilizer,
from bridge, under subway wheel, or into oven door,
what does it matter? Hemingway, de Staël, Jarrell,
Rothko, Berryman, Jackson or Sylvia Doe, how can it
matter? One wearies, that is all there is to say.

It is not all. One wearies; but one has to pace,
from within, the soft perimeters, night after night,
armed, sentinel, attendant. One must cock ear for
the old mole in the cellarage. Let it be neurones
gone berserk, or too much alcohol, one is obliged
contractually to mount constant watch against it.

2

And still it comes, in every sense. There is no stop-
ping it. Longing to find a way, one stumbles into
bed, and implicates another sack of skin, two skin-
sacks scandalously intricate. But, after that shell
game, the touted ten or twenty seconds shoot themselves,
punctual, inevitable as a philosopher's *Spaziergang*.

The dead cry all night long. Emptied and silent,
- leached, two skin-sacks loll among the bedclothes while
the moon slides over them. But that? That is not
the moon, it is a failing yellow bulb in the entryway

outside the window. . . . Hell has no need of hounds
to bound it. All bodies lie, at last, flat cut-outs,

flat, silhouettes scissored out of life by accidents
of time and circumstance, impenetrable, black
on white. One says one wearies of such jabber, such
bloat indulgence. One wishes it were otherwise, and
paces to and fro inside oneself, defending, trying to
defend. All night he keeps on burrowing, down under.

Une Semaine de Bonté
Hommage à Max Ernst

1 Sunday

Once, in a summer season, they intertwined, then
slept, exposed, upright, upon a wafer ledge, arranged,
it might be said, in a mimetic trustfulness, though
separated from the congeries of beasts which could
have warned them, should prefigured fissures widen.

But that was then, and this is now, whence issues
the punitive hairbrush, set with rusty needles, for
the shaved heads must be scraped down through their
scalps, until the skin slides off the skulls, leaving
a bare bone-ground for working by relentless harrows.

2 Monday

Wounds beget wounds: as what he said to her, and what
she did that day, and what they told us afterward,
which is why the flayed brain flickers on and off,
sending absolutely alien sensations and ideas abroad,
a ricochet of shreds and patches in the underground.

And the elephantine monsters, at long last, arrived,
drugged, muttering, all autumn long, clustering around
the bolted door, these, dispossessed, these, broken,
these, confounded, faintly roaring for asylum in her
bronze breasts, down under dark nipples dribbling lymph.

3 Tuesday

Even if the space A and the space B should be, in fact,
identical, for X to travel, at time t_1, from B to A,
and for Y to travel, at time t_1, from A to B, produces
an impasse, if one is the ordinary, God, who glances
down, at time t_n, to contemplate his worms in rut.

In his indifference lodges, precisely, our salvation.
For then blizzards may drift, at will, implacable,
between B and A, and A and B, which, at time t_{n+1},
abruptly levitate all misery, conferring freedom, even,
while the cold corrects (X, Y) into a single icicle.

4 Wednesday

Myopically squinting, through one's dusty past, at
the whatness of one's selfhood, one is distracted
by a black mote that keeps floating back and forth
across one's retina, until, outraged into elevated
brows, one demands the disposition of this animal.

It is allowable to leaf through travel books, then
plummet into sleep, and dream one's dreams, even should
the Laotian girl whose body one was about to pene-
trate, head first, diving, become a shaft of sharp
light, fracturing memory across mortalities of clocks.

5 Thursday

Let A conduct himself toward Z in the modality p,
let Z conduct herself toward A in the modality q,
then ((p implies q) implies (q implies p)) if and only
if ((((p and Z) implies q)) implies ((q and A) implies
p))), which, if true, yields up L, a language.

Ah, but the bottles keep smalling, the long nights
shortening, old wrinkled gonads, playing hard at hearts,
fail to make accordions of mattresses, wherefore, as
usually happens, ((not-p and Z) implies (not-q and A)),
and so there is no L, and Z and A are equi-equidistant.

6 *Friday*

It scarcely could be affirmed that the world stood
on edge, to watch that odd convergence of two entities,
sidling, like pessimistic explorers, lost in furs,
seeking insanely to touch gloves, across divaricating
floes of ice, at minus sixty-nine, among the penguins.

How unjust to have to give back what you never owned
to own, but guessed they had handed you, or, pale with
passion, begged you to believe you had been born with,
but of course the title had to be a total fraudulence,
since to be owned is not a proper property of persons.

7 *Saturday*

At the red bull's-eye of the ritual pillow fight,
whitened white with white of feather, they paused,
suddenly enraged, glaring across the living cell, and
recognized each other, eye for eye for eye for eye,
and someone, perhaps it was both, snapped off the switch.

A febrile hand or two contracted all those eyes to zeroes,
after which, feathers gave way to scabrous fingernails,
and these, in turn, to blood, and bone, and marrow,
as each fought the other down into the dizzy absolutes,
of which neither dreamed they might be merely in the mind.

9 August, 1976

II

A Cage for Loulou

¿por qué?

Into paint will I grind thee, my bride!

Being too idle to confirm it, I desire
to believe it was a parrot or a parrakeet
he fancied, to keep by him, in old age.
I want to picture him, letting it loose
across his writing-table, late at night.

Perhaps it pissed and shat the pages he
was struggling with, or shoved its beak into
the ink-stand, or scrabbled up his documents,
one bright eye blinking up toward his eye,
that blinked back, lourd of lid. "What you

and I can say, we ought to say together.
I, too, can speak." A human, writing, an
avian, collaborating, what could be a more
connubial arrangement, what more opulently
metaphorical? I wish to envy him: it seems

so much more spiritual than old apples, or
real scorpions, in desk-drawers. But: come to
think, the bird was dead and taxidermidized,
lice copulated in its fur, it was, for him,
an object, a model he required, for his art.

*   *   *   *   *   *   *

1

Caged in a wickerwork of pointless letters,
Loulou, occasionalist, considers choice:
to sing, to jabber, to nobble, to sleep. . . .

Wise voices chant: Faith is a great force.
Loulou's claw fidgets the wet confection
of a wafer: Loulou's mind considers. . . .

O the odor, O the odor, O the odor, O!
the stench of all those moments unconcatenated!
Loulou, occasionalist, grapples the nulliverse. . . .

Wake, Loulou, wake. Think, Loulou, think.
Act, Loulou, act. Strain eastward on your
westward-sailing galley, to your chain's end. . . .

—Good god good god good god good god:
the newspeak of the nightingale, Loulou,
publishes your epitaph without your name.

2

Do you love Loulou, Loulou?
—How could I not not?

Are you loved, Loulou?
—The drains are blocked.

Do you love, Loulou?
—In one dimension, only.

(Go: gather up the droppings,
comb carefully the coat,

pick out the nits, this
passing hour also will pass.)

Every tomorrow is a Sunday.
—One loves what one has to have to.

3

Stuffed thick with sticky nerve-spaghetti,
gasping all night long at the horny gates
of dream, what will you confess now, Loulou,
to exculpate your lost imbroglio?

—I feel like a raw egg eating half
of my non-existent brother (without shell).
Is it possible to commit suicide
by swallowing oneself (with shell, or

without?)? Is it possible to swallow one-
self without committing suicide (without
shell, or with?)? After inquests, truths:
for the embryo aborted, and furred clouds

divaricated, like curtains at a play. Since
infancy, nothing but rain, Loulou: what else
could brush up into praise but this tranquillity
of stained, old, glassy grass, this ground?

1.1   Loulou remembered is Loulou dead.

1.2   Loulou dead is Loulou remembered.

1.21   Being remembered and being dead are one.

2.1   There is no 2.1.

3.1   "   "   "   " .

3.2   And the damp hair of dusk goes dragging
       across the world that is without, within.

3.21

5

If Loulou had had pockets, what might not have dropped
from them?

The eyeballs, marinated in a sauce of time, leak desiccated
rods and cones, at every glance.

But that is all in order, as it should be. . . . Should it be?

Against these militant baffles, on the other hand, there
are no counter-measures yet devised. . . . Open: shut:
open: shut: open: shut: shut:. . . . like independent gills.

LOST,
amid the clatter of a shopfront,objects,coffee-mills,
dressmakers' dummies,advertisements for Sapolin,but objects,
some reflected,some refracted,some absorbed,some in the
glass,some on the glass,some behind the glass,some before
the glass,but objects,all gone from mind.

. . . .

How, then, is one to decode, much less contrive you, Loulou?

—Ah Loulou, Loulou! All that of your self is visible,
before the obsolescent banquet starts, is, simply, you,
upright, unpocketed, poll sidewise tilted, feathers, mud,
bemusement. . . .
But that is not you, Loulou, that is the me of you.

6

What do you remember, Loulou, what?
Do you remember those five fingers,
over your head, over, stroking, slow?

Do you remember those five fingers
(Do you remember, Loulou, do you?)
deep in your belly, ruffling you?

Do you remember those five fingers
carrying you, on their tips, away?
(How do you remember, Loulou, how?)

Can you remember, Loulou, can you?
Can you remember those five fingers
that you bit to blood, to free yourself?

7

Confabulate the history of Loulou.
—And incriminate myself?

Then Loulou is without a history?
—Conceivable.

A pastlessness in furious flight?
—Toward the grave.

The history of Loulou must divulge.
—A *chiquenaude*.

8 (*variazioni sul tema di Beckett*)

Have you discovered, Loulou, your true refuge?
This cage of syllables, perhaps, defines it?
Are you, at last, content? Hegira ended, all
now gone from mind, and another keeper, or none?

It is the shape only of a step, one step more,
as far as to that slow black ruin to which all
must come. Your cloth descends on you, caged
in the cage you carry yourself in, through time.

The slow black must descend, as the cloth does.
Unhappiness must reign again, and joy dissolve
in vanished dream. Is this your refuge, Loulou?
All gone into dream, never but imagined, all those

years of days that had to be endured before this
day, those journeys, that earth, this burlap sky?

40

9

—Once upon a time (*Begin!*), a morning, an instant, a moment,
of a day, an hour, somebody screamed, and deep from out of
the broom-closet, unspeakable uterus, a convolved cortex
rolled, writhing, bursting, full-term, breathless, for it
was the middle of the summer, the height of summer, years
ago, in Ohio, in August, in Ohio, years ago, in summer, a war
just ended, all the lawns in weeds, and all the heroes sagging
homeward, and in the crinkled water of the creek, down at
the bottom of the garden, catfish, tepidly exciting themselves,
slithering along the sliminess of dark brown stones.

—And one bird, one, gracing the sapling planted flag-like
in the front yard, one bird kept calling, slowly, slowly:
Loulou, one bird, insisting, nominating it, Loulou, one bird,
one dove, one pigeon, cooing, and they picked their eyes up
off the floor, and said, The name must have to be Loulou,
and then they knelt, as if reprieved, before the tunnel
of the telephone, and called the operator, who materialized
the hearse, which whispered rubber wheels and hairy bearers:
but one hero, dubious, arriving late, rubbed his medals
with his hands, fiercely (*End!*), challenging that one bird.

Is this, then, the history of Loulou?
—Tropically.

10

So small a body, Loulou, and so fine of
texture, one feared it could be rendered one-
dimensional by merely being looked at. . . .

No, no. Not even in a studio light. Now,
oscillate the poles of nudity, posing,
opposing, before a sentience of easels. . . .

All stemmed from that indulgence, so clear,
yet so dysnatural, to cherish arousing them
from deep within that icy field of force!

O Loulou, Loulou! playing among scissors,
razors, knives. . . ! Broad daylight is too harsh
for so much execution! Triple-lock away

unwanted children, dehydrate all the secret
pools, and tape, across the red, glum lips,
placards. . . . O how the lights must kill

themselves, Loulou, over whole your smallest
body! For all that, the caduceus must be
pulled down, flapping, a flag, a kind of voice,

at evening, must be reeled in like a fish,
a maiden drifting to her death, pulled down,
folded up, and put away. The moon affirms

the deed. So small a body, and so upright
with despair, pedaling itself along, tautened
under such an agony of baggage, agglutinated

volumes of disgust, from so far back what
child could count it out? But in nightmare
only dare one venture to begin the grasping,

the endurance of that regress, that descent
of Loulou, pedaling, into the farthest past,
enacting once again the saga of your origin. . . .

11

But, justly proposed, who is Loulou?
And who is there can give an answer?
Might it, perhaps, be the sun, sky high,
call him *apotheosis of an old felicity*,
call him *sacred zenith of the yellow
light*, call him *that notorious diurnal
oracle*, riding easily over the desertedness
of a dusty, fractionated human playground
haunted by ghosts of grizzled trolls?

—But must we lift our eyes, like that?
Must we use words that make us blush?
Must we stalk our eyes into the azure
to define you, or trace you out in fuzzy
figures of a distance: you, untagged item
in a warehouse of forgotten inventories,
you, angel of a disused paradise?

No, not the sun, even, in his whole nakedness,
is equipped, Loulou, to tell you who you are.

12

. . . . Always, shut the windows, and the walls, folded
like hands between clenched knees, a space collapsed
upon itself. Green grass, a meadow, on the wall,
a clearing, in a grove of trees, and, in the middle

of that lucid space, there, freshly dug, an open
grave, to contemplate. . . . The casually laundered air
of early morning, sun-struck, stings with a thin
venom. . . . The cage, draped in its crackled cloth,

the heart within the cage, the bird within the bird's
heart's heart, deaf, inaudible, remote, complete. . . .
Whoever undertakes to study out that bird, must pay.
There will be walls, and tears, and ugliness, in that

disordered polyhedron of choked sinks and dirty glass. . . .
Loulou, Loulou, Loulou! as if the iteration of a name
might so distend the globe as to persuade it to give
birth to one, just one, one bright miraculous event —

13

Nature admits no miracles. Climbing against
its will, the tributary incense dawdles, like

the hesitations of a pencil in a child's
hand, pondering contours of a maze, awaiting

death. Swords, idly scabbarded, attend
this divestiture, this baroque, disquiet rest.

* * * * * * *

Against Loulou, the spirit shrivels
into numbness, under coldest ice.

Against the spirit, Loulou searches,
with fitful beak, a lifted wing.

1 May 1976

III

The Cicatrice Tries
to Come of Age

Bastille Day

Reading, quizzing myself, moving about, washing
dishes, glancing through glass at the blue
day, or the grey, depending, gazing at the gay
sun or the bad rain, scared by leaves turned white
by wind, answering or speaking to the telephone,
making the bed, doing the laundry, going out in shoes
to explicate, with briefcase, Dante to the young,

I find myself, as in the dreams I dream, asleep,

a pilgrim in the labyrinthe I connived at, lost
among the murals, my nerves twitching to hard lines
that hurt my eyes, or soothed, sometimes, by soft
unexpected colors that mollify and stroke my mind,
until, invariably, running my skull against a wall,
I recognize you raw, as that strict memory that brings
me to myself, and blocks all passages with snow.

Boolean Algebra

1

"Is it, in any sense, a personal world?"

The moon reiterates 'her' simple repertoire,
the sun, 'his,' also, and all the neuter sky.

Ambushes. Boredoms. Children, wondering.
So politicians dine. Executives negotiate.
Among the wastes, the poor compete with maggots.

(You.   I.   You.   I.   You.   I.   You.)

2

Hand in hand, siblings infest the forest,
following delusive clues, that's how it
begins. Looking without seeing. Fear is big.

44

"Nothing is anywhere, and nobody cares."
No doubt this general atmosphere of zero-sum
encourages frenetic playing at forbidden games.

Believing in belief. Such boulevards of bread!

3

Exchange occasionally occurs: *You-I: I-you*.
The offices are vacated that would concede

that love is apolitical. (The frozen tomb
of Julio and Romiette.) Where are the passports?

Eyes tangent among the censored, thin portfolios.

It makes an end of language, yes. "Go wash
your face, brush your teeth, and get to bed."

4

Society is a dreary assignation in between the
solitudes, is it not, my little lost one?
Tendons in strain, a wrestling bout, hot strife
of sexes, armed. Façades collapse. Faith
goes up in steam. Under wet flesh, innocent
flowers wilt. Legitimate currencies lose their
balance. Water tables sink below the bit.

5

Night is perfectly irrefutable, likewise day,
save to the blind. Not so. Actiniariae

and Echinoideae yearn with the tides.
"Go trim your nails, the bombs are falling."

If you must die, die spotless. Long ago

there was a green, a suave, svelte place.
(I.   You.You.   I.I.   You.)

6

"Only to comprehend that no surd has an end. . . ."

Commandeer a desk packed with grenades. Hunt
furiously. Do not jar or pull a pin.
A black light nullifies this narrowed iris.

Far out there in the dark of trees a lonely
Monarch, beating against the door, battering
a rusty wire-web, begging to come home.

7

(I   You.   You.   I.   You.   You I.)

Machine-guns, clothes-pins, carbon-paper.
Inventions, all those violent substitutes for tears.
"We went out to the park, carrying sandwiches."

Sat at a table, in among the flies and bees.
Kept ourselves going, as best we could. . . . . . .

Mortality awoke us, like a pistol-shot.

Peripatetic Diagnosis

Agoraphobia, no: I enjoy the grace of spaciousness.
But not the other, either, since to be enclosed composes
me among my selves.

Walking to the grocery, turning over, as one must, the
leaves of the catalogue of my disorders, I stopped
short at wrist-watches.

For an instant I deployed myself as chief conductor in
a horological museum, compelling every piece to mark
the tyranny of cesium.

No good. A bird kept improvising, on a branch, above me,
two cars angrily disputed the intersection, and asymmetry
is sin transliterated geometrically.

Forcing a right angle, I had to think of you, and how I
used to come to you by deviant paths, that guided me more
truly than this proper.

All day long I have been browsing in that deadly book,
trying in vain to fix upon the section that displays the
gift that poisoned us.

Disorders of the Interface

Things shift uneasily, disoriented
beasts, circling inside their spaces.
The landscape only seems to blend,
glimpsed from behind a moving window.

A woman, straddling a man in a late
bed, rising and sinking, suddenly flung
back her head, and showed the face
Bernini gave Teresa. But of what use

was that? She could not see herself,
because her eyes were closed, and he,
though open-eyed, was living elsewhere.
We know how many-valued these expressions

can be. Faces are voids at the centers
of universes, but what if the given
universe happens to be being hammered
to the breaking point? There is more

than enough space, in time, for random
spades to excavate surprises, rubbish
of petty murders long forgotten, or else
never known. And is a look that is seen

by no one, still a look? Yes, and no.
It is an uncanny thing to contemplate
droplets of whisky, querulous as
old men out of Beckett, trailing down

the inner sloping of a shot-glass,
scared of that great sea of amber
underneath them, twitching galvanically
every time they barely graze its sur-

face, struggling not to be absorbed.
Language, it must be admitted, seems
to work, sometimes, and motion is not
illusory always, and leaves that once

were buds drop off their trees to join
their predecessors in that gutter
that will trip you if you fail to
notice it. It is a human act, to touch,

and then let go, to talk, and then fall
silent, to couple, and then become
estranged. The edges of things keep
trying introspective, paltry gestures.

Wittgenstein and Language

"—As if I ever wanted to command the oboe. . . !"
Yet you have always, very secretly, desired,
containing in yourself such quantities of air,

as to keep alive a fear of going crazy, some-
one to go and fetch an oboe into which you might,
at long length, empty out yourself, and so

assuage your fear of going crazy. (It's nothing
but a simple double-reed, audible above the ag-
glomerated orchestra, the A by which the strings

attune themselves, an A, the only A, a desolated
A, sounding before the disorder of the concert
starts, Boieldieu, Chopin, Dvořák, Elgar, de

Falla. . . .) No. Better become the oboe and be
played by a man whose beard is reddish, a man
of fingers, a man whose trouser-legs, correctly

bent, delineate a sitfast folding chair. This
is the music, which both follows and precedes
you. "I am its instrument. I perform. I *speak*—"

The Cicatrice Tries to Come of Age

1

Recovering from illness can sometimes seem
more nearly like an exploration than a
homecoming, if only because the stage-set
into which one wakens, and the faces,
masked, flowering down like surgeons in
a doubtful film, for all the similarities

that make one want to wave, sit up, and cry,
Hello, I'm back again! are polarized
and filtered, cut, and mixed, so as to dis-

combobulate one's first naïve delight,
and leave one with the feeling that
familiarity following excess abruptly

serves up the most complex of puzzles;
and so one sits a long while, hunched
on the side-stairs of the belvedere of
sentiment, fiddling one's sense of where
and who one is, as if one were an optical
confusion, a spider-cube that will not yield

its contours, no matter which way it is
turned. . . . It would, at just this moment, be
incorrect to conclude that things are other
than felicitous. Shifting the furniture
makes hollows, and the space a limb once
occupied refuses to behave like a space.

The hollows must be experienced, the space
be made to be receptive. Thought, after
all is said, will follow fingertip more
obediently than any soldier follows orders.
And the mind, that old hole, into which,
soon or late, the world discharges itself,

all the solids and liquids of existence,
all the snot, shit, semen, spit, piss,
tears, lymph, pus, and blood of our corporeal
impieties, compacted into spectral bundles,
bags, or sacks, in that strange no place,
the mind worries its words, and, worrying,

worries itself a world, as a terrier, flat
in a corner of the dining-room, honing
his teeth, satisfying his gut, creating his
pleasure, an intensely private renovation
of his cosmos, worries his allotted bone.

2

Recollection is, by definition, painful, is
a tonality, a minor key of being, to the effects
of which this theme that happens to invent itself
is categorically irrelevant. All the past
is a disconcerted clutter of lives, of doors,
tables, beds, lamps, clothes, old books, dirty

dishes, dirty windows, broken toys and toilets,
a decaying house perpetually in process of
vacation. The mind keeps being led back there,
especially following failure, because the path
has been mapped into the branchings of the blood.
And so, even if thought does follow fingertip,

so also will fingertip tag after thought, or,
habitude, seductive drug, keeps tempting
language to gnaw itself, as if it were a wound
one might be able to forget, except that gnawing,
keeping the blood oozing, guarantees a focus,
a graveyard to keep digging sentimental holes in.

Still, in the worst moments, things keep
beckoning, handkerchiefs soliciting the corners
of the eyes, to wipe away a natural afterbirth.
Is there a dialect(ic) of redemption? I am not I
because my little dog knows me. I am I
because I inexplicably take up my little dog

and kiss him on the snout. Such unpremedi(t)ated
gestures, aimed into the world, keep naming us
to ourselves. Most structures seem to want to
hang together, through tidal waves, earthquakes,
eclipses of the sun or moon, even, perhaps,
the ticking of the clock. Whatever happens

has to become a member of the family. One
wrestles with a yearning to bestow, upon this
moment or that, a patent of nobility, and often
one yields, but, in the latitude experience affirms,
the effort has to fail, the body comes up short
against a stony present tense, and so the mind

must follow suit. No: all these paths of memory
eventually shrivel out of sense, dwindling from
artery to capillary, thence to disordered overgrowth,
as the traffic that used to pass makes other paths,
and these are weathered into flat forgottenness.

Retrospective

I have given up contemplating murder now,
the meadows of my life having become honeycombed
with ambidextrous burials, as I look back,
so many living roots have been attacked, wherefore
among those hopeful, these dejected flowers.

A spider drops down on my finger, as I lie
in bed, reading, and so, reminded of having
dreamt of you, I consider it again, already
settled, the question I propound myself, whether
to linger on my human hand, or run away.